A
High
Schooler's
Guide to Java

{

Rithul Bhat;

}

Rithul Bhat

A High Schooler's Guide to Java, First Edition

Copyright © 2024 by Rithul Bhat

To Appa, Amma, & My Teachers

Thank you for always guiding & supporting me

Preface

After reading numerous books and studying for countless hours trying to understand concepts related to computer science, I decided that it was time to create a comprehensive book that would give my future peers a headstart in their learning journey of Java. While teachers could explain concepts and textbooks could give examples, nothing really voiced examples and definitions quite like a brand-new student would understand. So who better to explain it than a high school student himself?

This book serves to solve all of those problems. It does not assume that you have ANY prior computer science knowledge, and it will explain all the fundamental concepts you will need to know in an easy-to-understand manner. For those who already have a head start in these fields, this book will provide you with an even stronger structure for all your future endeavors.

"A High Schooler's Guide to Java" has chapters that each outline a major concept of object oriented programming. Each chapter has a segment that will help you understand the concept so you will be ready for your high school career! Note that most of these concepts originate from the AP Computer Science A curriculum. By the end of this book, you will not only become a better coder, but a better debugger, problem solver, and get good grades in school!

Final note - this book's main purpose is to give you a **surface understanding** of most of the **fundamental Java concepts**. Once you understand the basic elements of these concepts, you can go more in-depth in the future! The best part of it all: it is condensed into 100 pages, not only maximizing your time, but helping you learn faster as well. Hope you enjoy it!

- Rithul Bhat

Table of Contents

Chapter 1: How Should I Use This Book?

The first thing to understand while using this book is that it is made specifically for students in school who are trying to learn more about computer science and Java. Therefore, the book is centered around high school Java topics and is structured as a student might see.

Use the **Glossary** at any point during the book if there is terminology you do not understand.

Structure To Remember

While reading through this book and learning new concepts, there is a **structure** that you should look out for in every chapter so that you know the purpose of the content that is being presented to you. The way the book is laid out is made so that it will create a structured learning path for you to fully grasp the Java idea you are learning! Take a look at the breakdown below and keep this page handy in case you want to remember the order:

1. Chapter header

2. Definition of concept in an easy-to-understand explanation

3. Examples of the concept (Vocab will be **bolded**)

4. Check for understanding

When you read this book, have Eclipse (the place where you will type your code) open so you can keep up with the code and examples. We will set up Eclipse in a few pages.

Chapter 2: Getting Started With Java

What is Java?

In short, Java is a programming language. That's obvious - but what is it that these programming languages do? First, it's important to note that Java follows OOP, or Object Oriented Programming. This means that everything you code in Java will revolve around objects.

After being released in 1995, Java quickly rose to the top of the software world, becoming one of the MOST used coding languages of all time. Java is now used in almost everything you see online, especially to create dynamic websites. Java is also the core of desktop and mobile apps. Whether it is games, utilities, or web development, Java is all around us, which is why this book will not only make you good at school but will build an awesome foundation for your future as well.

Before you learn any Java or start coding in Java, you need to get a few things ready in order to maximize your experience.

Where Do I Write My Code?

With most programming languages, you can either write your code in a terminal or an IDE (Integrated Development Environment). A terminal is a text-based software that can execute code directly to your computer. This is also known as Powershell or console. If you go to your computer's "Search" bar, click on the terminal and get a feel for what it is like.

While a terminal is a great way to code and practice, it is best to use an IDE when learning and testing new things out. An IDE, which stands for Integrated Development Environment, is basically an editor for all your code. It can import, compile, run, and debug your code all in one place.

The first step to learning Java is to understand where and how to write your code, so it is time to install an IDE on your computer. There are several IDEs you can use, however the most popular Java-based IDE is called Eclipse. Eclipse is the primary platform used in schools and the workforce as well, which is why all the examples in this book will be based in the Eclipse software. Please type the examples in your Eclipse while we are going through it - it makes learning a lot easier.

If you already have an IDE installed, skip to the next chapter. If not, take a look below for download instructions.

How To Install An IDE

Read the following instructions in order to get your IDE set up on your computer.

1. Go to your default web browser (Google, Safari, Edge, etc) and search up "Eclipse IDE Download". (www.eclipse.org)

2. Click on the link that says "Eclipse Downloads | The Eclipse Foundation". If you do not see this, click on another link you think is correct (sometimes varies from computer to computer).

3. Click on the Download button. On the dropdown, there are 2 options. If you are working on a MacOS device, select AArch64. If you are using any other device, select x86_64. These are the different types of software needed for your computers.

4. Complete the rest of the steps that your computer instructs you to do. After it is complete, open your Eclipse Application by either searching for it or double-clicking on the Eclipse icon on your desktop.

First Java Program

Now that your IDE is set up and your computer is updated, it is time to write your first program! Here is a quick step by step guide:

1. Open your Eclipse IDE. Upon entering, select the directory you want to work with. This is where all of your files will download on your computer.

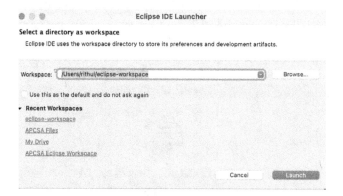

2. Now, you should see a blank window to the left sidebar, where you will click "Create a Java Project".

3. Name the project "First Java Program" at the top of the dialog window. In the section that says JRE, you can see the version of Java you are using. Don't touch any of that for now. We will keep it default.

4. Click on the Next button, and hit Finish. You have created your first project! Now let's write some code.

5. On the left sidebar, you can see all the various Java Projects you have created in Eclipse. You should see the "First Java Program" folder. Click on it. There will be an additional folder called "src". Right-click on the folder and make a new class.

6. In the dialog window, write FirstProgram for the name of the class. Then, click the checkbox that says "public static void main...". We will talk more later about what these words mean. Go to the next page for a visual.

7. Click Finish. You have created your first .java file! Navigate to line 6 and write the following code to print out a message!

```
System.out.println("Hello World!");
```

Complete picture of the class itself for your reference in the next page.

```
J  *FirstProgram.java  ×
1
2  public class FirstProgram {
3
4⊖      public static void main(String[] args) {
5              // TODO Auto-generated method stub
6              System.out.println("Hello World!");
7      }
8  }
```

8. Now, click the green play button at the top of your window. It should be located at the navigation bar. This is the Run button. Whenever you want to rerun and execute your code, you should click on this button.

9. Take a look at the bottom of your screen after clicking on the button. There should be a tab called the console. The console is where all your input and output will be facilitated inside of Eclipse. You should see the text Hello World! printed in the tab. It will most likely be at the bottom of your screen. If it isn't, click on the search bar and search for "console (general)".

Console ×
<terminated> FirstProgram [Java Ap
Hello World!

10. Congrats! You have completed your first java program!

Chapter 3: Data Types & Objects

Now that you know how to create a Java project and class, it is time to learn the most basic fundamental concepts of Java. Everything in computer science revolves around information - where information is stored, how information is stored, why information is stored in some places compared to others, etc.

What are Data Types?

The textbook explanation of a data type is a way of holding on to a piece of memory. Basically, it means that data types hold values that we want to store in our programs. There are many different ways to hold values with data types, which is why they are split mainly into 2 groups.

The first group consists of something called primitive types. These types come default in any Java program. There are 8 types of these primitives, and they each hold a different type of value. When working with data types, it is best to use the data type that best holds the value needed.

In addition, each data type has a different size than the other. The unit of measurement for memory size is bits. 8 bits are in 1 byte.

The more bytes a primitive has, the more values it can hold. Here is the table of all 8 primitives, how much they hold, and what values they can hold (notice they are all lowercase):

Table	Size	Value	Range
boolean	1 Bit	True/False	N/A
byte	1 Byte	Integers	-128 to 127
short	2 Bytes	Integers	-32768 to 32767
int	4 Bytes	Integers	-2147483648 to 2147483647
long	8 Bytes	Integers	-9.223372E18 to 9.223372E18 - 1
float	4 Bytes	Decimals	6-7 Decimals
double	8 Bytes	Decimals	<15 Decimals
char	2 Bytes	Letter	One single letter

Declaration & Initialization (And other vocab)

It's important to understand some vocabulary in every chapter so that it is easier to grasp certain Java concepts. One thing to understand is **declaration**. This means a certain data type is created. This means that you, as the programmer, create a new variable that has the potential to hold values in the future.

When you assign a value to that declared variable, it is called **initialization**.

The name that you give to a certain object is called a **reference**. Every single time a reference is given a new value, it is called **reassignment** (The first value is the initialization).

All of the bolded words are ones you should know well, so if you need extra clarification, take a look at the **glossary**.

Examples of Primitive Types

The best way to learn about most concepts in this book is to play around in Eclipse and gain an understanding of the capabilities of each and every feature. Let's take each data type one by one and understand how they work. Go back into your "First Java Program" file and write this there.

Starting with the **boolean**. We know they can hold true and false values, so let's run it through Eclipse. In order to **declare** a boolean data type, write the following code -

```
boolean myFirstBoolean;
```

Notice a few things here. First of all, we are creating a boolean, so we write "boolean" first in our line of code. Next, we can write the **reference**, or name, of the data type. I named mine myFirstBoolean. Keep in mind that I used something called **camelCase**, which is a style that programmers in Java use for all reference names.

CamelCase has the first word all lowercase, and then the first letter of every word after capitalized. It is recommended to follow these styles, or **syntax** when writing code. Writing with good syntax allows your code to be easy to read and fix! In order to **initialize** your boolean write -

```
myFirstBoolean = false;
```

You can also declare and initialize values at the same time. For a boolean, for example, you could do this -

```
boolean myFirstBoolean = false;
```

Now that you understand this pattern, the next 7 primitives should be the same! Let's take a look at data type int. It will be the same pattern everywhere. Take a look -

```
[data type] [reference] = [value]

int exampleInt = 25;
```

In the last statement, we declared and initialized the variable all in one line! Play around with the values. Notice if you go above the values it can hold (you can reference the table) then Eclipse will give you an error. Tinkering around with the code on your own is the best way to learn!

Other integer-related data types include the **byte, short, int, and long**. Using the same pattern, type the following lines of code into Eclipse -

```
byte myFirstByte = 15;

short myFirstShort = 15000;

int myFirstInt = 1500000000;

long myFirstLong = 15000000000;
```

Everything seems to work right?? No! While the short and int are fine with this declaration, the long seems to have some kind of problem. Make sure you write this into Eclipse to learn it best!

When you declare a long, it wants you to put an "L" after the value if it exceeds the value of an int.

If you delete one 0 from your long value, there is no error, as it is still in the int range. However, the moment it goes above that, there is an error. Type the following code to fix it.

```
long myFirstLong = 15000000000L;
```

Now that we covered all of the whole-number data types, let's go over the last 3. A float is the first kind of decimal value holder we will discuss. Just like a long, it requires a letter after the value, but in this case, it is an F. You can use either a lowercase or uppercase F. Here is what a float looks like when it is declared and initialized.

```
float myFirstFloat = 25.50F;
```

A double is kind of like an int, except it takes decimal values as well. It does not require a letter - just put the number and you are fine.

```
double myFirstDouble = 25.50;
```

Finally, there is a char, which is just a single letter assigned to the reference. Notice how we use single quotes in this syntax.

```
char myFirstChar = 'r';
```

From the following examples, you can see how each of the variables is brought into our projects, and how we can use each. If you want to print out some of these values, use the println command we used before, and just put the reference between the parenthesis, and the output will be in the console. For example -

```
System.out.println(myFirstDouble);
```

Arithmetic Operations With Primitives

Now that we know basic information regarding primitives, let's do some math with them. Just like the basic math you know, we can add(+), subtract(-), multiply(*), and divide(/). We can use these operators to do math in our programs.

If we want to find the remainder of a number, we use modulus(%). For example, 12 % 5 would be 2, because that is the remainder of the division problem.

Examples of Arithmetic Operations

Let's continue with our First Java Project files. We will use the previous data types that we initialized in the following programs.

Beginning with addition (you can use either example):

```
int add = myFirstShort + myFirstInt;

int add = myFirstInt + myFirstByte;
```

As you can see, another variable is being declared and initialized here to hold this sum value. You will notice that you will have to do this for all of the future operations as well. To print the value, you can either print the add variable or just place the entire operation in the print method.

```
System.out.println(add);

System.out.println(myFirstShort +
myFirstInt);
```

Using the same pattern, let's repeat this for subtraction, multiplication, division, and mod. Notice how I made add an int - you can change this at your discretion, but keep in mind you will get an error if you try putting a decimal value into an int!

Use the following lines of code to understand when you do and do not use certain data types in situations.

```
double subtract = myFirstLong -
myFirstDouble;

int multiply = myFirstShort *
myFirstInt;
```

```
double divide = myFirstLong /
myFirstDouble;

double mod = myFirstFloat %
myFirstByte;

System.out.println(subtract);

System.out.println(myFirstLong -
myFirstDouble);

System.out.println(multiply);

System.out.println(myFirstShort *
myFirstInt);

System.out.println(divide);

System.out.println(myFirstLong /
myFirstDouble);

System.out.println(mod);

System.out.println(myFirstFloat %
myFirstByte);
```

If you take a look at the console, you will notice that each pair of print statements prints the same value, so it is up to your discretion as a programmer which line of code you want to use in the future.

Keeping this in mind, add a "//" before the lines you do not want to use. This will make that line a **comment**. A comment is a line of code that will not execute when you click the run button. They will prove to be very helpful to you as a programmer in the future.

I prefer to just print one variable, as it is cleaner and makes the code easier to understand.

Keep tinkering around with these operations and numbers to see what values are displayed, what each operation does, and what data types can correspond to certain operations.

Take a look at the next page for the entire class-

```java
 1
 2  public class FirstProgram {
 3
 4      public static void main(String[] args) {
 5          // TODO Auto-generated method stub
 6          System.out.println("Hello World!");
 7
 8          boolean myFirstBoolean = false;
 9          byte myFirstByte = 15;
10          short myFirstShort = 15000;
11          int myFirstInt = 1500000000;
12          long myFirstLong = 15000000000L;
13          float myFirstFloat = 25.50F;
14          double myFirstDouble = 25.50;
15          char myFirstChar = 'r';
16
17          int add = myFirstByte + myFirstInt;
18          double subtract = myFirstLong - myFirstDouble;
19          int multiply = myFirstShort * myFirstInt;
20          double divide = myFirstLong / myFirstDouble;
21          double mod = myFirstFloat % myFirstByte;
22
23          String myFirstString = "I like Java";
24
25          System.out.println(add);
26          //System.out.println(myFirstByte + myFirstInt);
27
28          System.out.println(subtract);
29          //System.out.println(myFirstLong - myFirstDouble);
30
31          System.out.println(multiply);
32          //System.out.println(myFirstShort * myFirstInt);
33
34          System.out.println(divide);
35          //System.out.println(myFirstLong / myFirstDouble);
36
37          System.out.println(mod);
38          //System.out.println(myFirstFloat % myFirstByte);
39
40          System.out.println(myFirstString);
41      }
42  }
```

Reference Types

Now that you know all about primitive types, it's time to learn about **reference types.** Reference types, also known as object types, are data types that are linked to an object. Unlike primitives, object types are variables that have to be imported or created, and they are actually within something called a **class**. A class is located within a java file, just like the one you are writing in. A class is a blueprint that holds information and code to perform certain tasks.

The most common reference type in Java is called **String**. A String is an array of characters - so essentially any text field. Whenever you want to type anything text-related, it will be a string.

Normally, you would have to use an import statement in order to access String, but in our case, the Object class is automatically included in default Java files.

Reference Types are more of an advanced concept that you will understand more easily later on in this book. However, just so you know what a String looks like, here is the **declaration**, **initialization**, and **print** of a Java String -

```
String myFirstString = "I Like Java";

System.out.println(myFirstString);
```

Notice how we keep the same naming conventions as a normal data type, with camelCase. However, looking into the type itself, notice how String is capitalized, unlike any of the previous primitives. To set a value to a String, you must use double quotations. Simply put it around the value or text you want, and you're set.

Congratulations! You have finished your first content-related chapter. If you feel that you need to brush up on a few concepts, go back through the book and understand them, or search them online! Every chapter from now on will be a different Java project, This chapter was located in your First Java Program project.

Next, you will have a **Check For Understanding**. Normally, a check for understanding will be about 1-2 pages long. It will mostly have questions about what we just talked about, but will also have a few challenge questions at the end to get your gears turning. As we move on in chapters, there may be questions from old chapters to make sure that you retain most of this information!

Check For Understanding (Chapter 3)

1. Write code to declare a variable called "chapterFour" as a type of short. Do not initialize the variable.

2. Create an int called "sum" that adds 5 and 10 together. Print out "sum" to the console.

3. Print 70 modulus 3 in the console.

4. Declare and initialize a variable type char called "charS" and set the value to "S".

5. What is the name of the capitalization convention used on variable names?

6. If you had the value of 300.0, which data types could you use to hold these values?

7. What symbol do we find at the end of every statement in Java?

8. True or False: You must declare a variable before using it.

9. What is the difference between declaration and initialization?

Check For Understanding (Chapter 3 ANSWERS)

1. `short chapterFour;`

2. `int sum = 5 + 10;`

`System.out.println(sum);`

3. `System.out.println(70 % 3);`

4. `char charS = 'S';`

5. Camel Case

6. Double or Float (Decimal Value Holders)

7. A semicolon (;)

8. True. Without a declaration, the variable does not exist and will create an error in your code.

9. Declaration is when the variable/object is created, but not necessarily given a value. When a variable is given its first value, it is initialized.

Chapter 4: Writing Classes, Variables, & Methods

Now that you learned about data types and variables, it is time to put them to the test in some mini projects. However, there is some basic terminology you should understand. Create a new Java project called "Classes, Variables, and Methods". If you forgot how to do this, refer back to previous pages and retrace your steps. Now, let's write a class of our own.

Overview

A class is a blueprint that can create and manipulate objects to your benefit. In the last chapter, we created a simple class that could do arithmetic operations. As you become a more experienced programmer, you will notice all the sophisticated tasks a class can carry out.

Classes

Now that you have a quick debrief on what classes are, let's write a class of our own. When we usually create classes in our Java projects, there is a standard with most files. Most of your classes will contain code to program functions and actions.

Then, you will have a Runner class that takes this code and puts it to use. To better understand these concepts, let's start by creating a Movie class.

Right-click on your src file and create a new class as last time, except this time do not click the checkbox for a main method. Name the class "Movies".

Now that we have an empty class, let's add some variables that we might find associated with a movie. For the sake of this example, let's make 2 variables: one for the movie's name and one for the movie's rating.

```
String name = "Avengers";

double rating = 4.8;
```

However, once we create these variables, there can only be one value held at any time. To change this, we must create something called an object. The beauty of classes is their ability to provide a blueprint to create objects.

In context to this problem, you can imagine a single object to be a single movie. The object of a movie should have both a name and a rating. To make these objects, we have to create something called a **constructor** in the Movies class.

Constructors

Objects, as mentioned before, play a critical role in Java. However, in order to make our own objects, we must use/create something called a **constructor**. As its name suggests, a constructor is something that constructs objects!

After our previous variable declarations, write this code:

```
public Movies(){

}
```

If you notice, this exhibits the same pattern as seen in other structures. We have the word "public", and then the name of the class. Finally, we use brackets to enclose the constructor's content.

Now that we created a skeleton for the constructor, we need to actually create the commands for the object itself. To manipulate any data, we need to start by declaring the variables that they will be stored in.

Remember how we created those previous variables? We have to change these into something called **instance variables**. These variables are always associated with a certain object. In this case, we want the movie name and rating to be associated with a certain object, so this makes sense! Now we will create instance variables for our class.

To create an instance variable, we can just simply declare the variable without initializing it. **Change** the **previous** lines of code to this:

```
String name;

double rating;
```

Now that we have these variables ready for values to be inserted into them, we can implement them within our constructor. To make this constructor as simple as possible, we will simply make it assign the value of "Avengers" to the name and "4.8" to the rating.

If you notice, the only difference with the constructor is that now we are initializing our variables within the constructor. This will prove to be increasingly helpful in the future.

```
public Movies(){

    name = "Avengers";

    rating = 4.8;

}
```

Now that we have created a constructor that can create an object with data, we need to create actions that can change and manipulate this data. We call these actions **methods**, and we will write a few simple examples in the Movies class.

Methods

In order to make our class capable of actually doing anything, we must create a method inside of our Movies.java file. If you remember, the format to create a header for a method is

```
[public/private] [return type] [method
name](parameters)
```

```
public int intMethod()
```

In order to create our method, we will follow the same pattern. Together, we will create a method to print out the values of our movie to the console.

Let's take this one step at a time. We know we want our method to be accessible from other classes, so we must make it **public**. In addition, since the purpose of our method is to print something and not necessarily return it, our return type will remain **void**.

Finally, the name of our method - it is recommended that the name of your method reflects what your method actually does, so let's name the method **printMovie**. We will not have any parameters as the method itself is only printing the variable, not changing it.

```java
public void printMovie(){

    System.out.println("Movie Name: "
+ name);

    System.out.println("Movie Rating:
" + rating);

}
```

Notice the way we print the string here is the same way we printed our variables in the previous chapter. This method simply takes the Movie object we defined earlier and prints it to the console.

After writing this code, we have a constructor that creates data and a method to print the data. But how do we run the data? Remember, the only way to execute your data and program is through a Main method. It is a good practice to have your Main method in a separate **Runner Class.**

The Runner Class

Now, create another class called "Runner". Right click the folder on the right and navigate to New/Class. For this class, click the checkbox to make the main method when creating the file.

Most projects from now on will have a separate runner class to execute all files to keep a structured and organized coding environment. This is what your class should look like -

```java
1
2 public class Runner {
3
4     public static void main(String[] args) {
5     }
6
7 }
```

The line of code you see on line 4 is called a method header. This outlines everything that the method will do and the capabilities it has. The code inside the header is the body - it holds the actions that allow the method to do its job.

Let's analyze the meaning of each word in the header. If you do not understand what it means now, just get a basic understanding - you will understand the full meaning of them by the end of the book.

public means that this method can be accessed by other classes in the same project. They can simply call the method from another class in order to execute the file.

static means that this method is attached to the class itself, not an object. Once we want to access certain information about an object, we would create an instance method, but we will learn more about that later.

void means that this method does not specifically return any type. The alternative would be a certain data type being returned, like an int. In most situations, a main method will be void.

main is the name of the method itself and **String[] args** is something called a parameter, which is essentially the input that the method takes in. This input contains the information required to give an output in the method.

All of the information about the header stated will stay standard for most main methods, so try to get a surface understanding as well as you can.

Inside the Runner class, you should already have the main method included by default.. The first thing we need to do is create an object of type Movies. Once we can create this object, we can print its properties.

When we make an object, we have to use the **new** keyword. Whenever this keyword is used, it is said that the object is **instantiated**, meaning that the object has been given a state to be in. Here is the basic structure of creating an object:

```
[Name of type] [name]= new [name of
type];
```

For the sake of this demonstration, we can assign the reference to the name "avengers", as that is the name of our movie. After the equals sign, we write new and Movies again before writing empty parenthesis since there were no parameters in our constructor in the Movies.java file.

```
Movies avengers = new Movies();
```

Now that the object has been instantiated, we can perform actions with it! Since we only programmed for one action in Movies, we can only call that one method. When calling an instance method, which is a method that is tied to a specific object, you have to first specify the name of that object, and then call the method for that object. Let's call printMovie for the test object.

```
avengers.printMovie();
```

Let's run the code! If you did everything correctly, we should see this in the console:

```
Movie: Avengers

Rating: 4.8
```

To better understand the process that went behind the scenes, we should trace the code. When we first ran the main method, the Avengers object with the type Movies was created. The compiler will go to Movies.java to make sure a constructor exists.

Once it found a viable constructor, it read the instructions in the constructor assigned to those objects. In the code, the name was assigned to the value of Avengers, and the rating was assigned to the value of 4.8!

Traveling back to the Runner class, the program called the public method printMovie, which was assigned to the Avengers object. Since the object contained the values of Avengers and 4.8, that is what it printed to the console!

More Constructors!

Now that we have made one constructor, let's make another one that creates another object! Go back into Movies, and below the old constructor, create the same thing. What happens?

It gives an error! Why? Because you cannot have the same constructor in the same class - there must be a change or difference in the parameters that are passed into the constructor.

Try this yourself, you already have the second constructor's base finished. Let's make this constructor take a String as a **parameter** and **reassign** the value of that String to remoteString. This will make a custom String print when this object is created.

Take some time to figure it out. Once you have tried a few times, take a look at the code below and compare.

```
public Movies(String movie, double
enterRating){

    name = movie;

    rating = enterRating;

}
```

Notice how you have to create a new variable in the parenthesis - this is called a parameter. We declare the variable here, but unlike a normal variable, we do not use a semicolon. We will do this for both the name and rating of the movie itself.

If you notice, this new constructor allows us to change the movie's values however we would like. In the body of the constructor, we reassign the value of custom to name and rating, which replaces the empty value it had before.

Can you figure out how to call the new constructor we just made? Follow the same pattern we did for the previous constructor - except now you must put a String as a parameter since that is how the constructor is defined.

After trying a few things out, refer to this code to compare. Make sure this code is in the Runner Class -

```
Movies spiderMan = new Movies("Spider
Man", 4.7);
```

Now, we have called the new constructor with the new
keyword, and since we put a parameter it will call the
custom version. Now, we must call the printMovie method
for the custom object as well:

```
spiderMan.printMovie();
```

Run the program. Wow! The new constructor is called and
our new movie is printed to the console. This project taught
you how to create different objects and use them to call
methods and variables. Here is the completed class and
console for your reference.

```
    Movies.java ×
1
2  public class Movies {
3
4       String name;
5       double rating;
6
7      public Movies() {
8           name = "Avengers";
9           rating = 4.8;
10      }
11
12      public Movies(String movie, double enterRating){
13           name = movie;
14           rating = enterRating;
15      }
16 |
17
18      public void printMovie() {
19           System.out.println("Movie Name: " + name);
20           System.out.println("Movie Rating: " + rating);
21      }
22 }
23
```

```
  1
  2 public class Runner {
  3
  4   public static void main(String[] args) {
  5
  6       Movies avengers = new Movies();
  7       Movies spiderMan = new Movies("Spider Man", 4.7);
  8
  9       avengers.printMovie();
 10       spiderMan.printMovie();
 11
 12   }
 13
 14 }
 15
```

```
Console X

<terminated> Runner (1) [Java Application] /Users/rithul/.p2/pool/plugins/org.eclipse.ju
Movie Name: Avengers
Movie Rating: 4.8
Movie Name: Spider Man
Movie Rating: 4.7
```

How Do You Tell Them Apart?

With so many names and code on your screen, do you know how to differentiate between classes, variables, and methods? The main answer lies in analyzing the naming conventions that go into these different structures.

For classes, you will always see the name start with a **capital letter**. For example, both ContentClass and Runner start with capital letters, so they are classes in your project. Other classes, such as String, are **wrapper classes** that are introduced from Java itself. Look at the glossary to learn more about wrapper classes.

For variables, as discussed before, will always be written in **Camel Case**, which makes it distinguishable from other Java types. In addition, the color coding on Eclipse makes it easy to understand what is what. If you look closely, all the variables in the ContentClass.java file are highlighted in blue. These subtle touches will allow you to tell the difference.

Finally, with methods, the most tell-tale sign to know it is a method is to look for **parenthesis**. For example, in our printString method, there was always a parenthesis after the call for any parameters. This is the easiest way to tell when something is a method.

In general, **color coding** on Eclipse is quite helpful when it comes to contrasting the different code you are working with. Classes and methods will always be black, variables will always be blue, and objects will also be blue, but italicized as well.

With everything in this chapter, you should be familiar with writing your own classes, creating constructors, writing simple methods, and ultimately executing all the code in the Runner class. If you are confused or need to take more time to understand, please do. These concepts, if known well, will make your Java experience a lot easier and more fun as well!

Check For Understanding (Chapter 4)

Create a new class CFU4 in your Eclipse Project to type this check for understanding in.

1. Declare and initialize an instance variable of type int. Start it to the value of 0 and name it myInt.

2. Create a constructor that takes one int as a parameter. Inside the constructor, change the value of myInt to whatever the parameter was.

3. Create a method that prints out the value of myInt.

4. Create an object called customInt of type CFU in the Runner class. Then, call the method to print out the value of customInt.

5. What is instantiation?

6. In the statement below, what is the class, method, object, and argument/parameter?

```
System.out.println("Chapter 4");
```

7. True or False: The main method is usually in your content class, while the actions defined are in the runner class.

8. True or False: You can identify classes by looking out for capital letters.

Check For Understanding (Chapter 4 ANSWERS)

The below images are the answers for questions 1 - 4 .

(The console should return "5", since my object was initialized to that value.)

```
      CFU4.java        *Runner.java  X
  1
  2  public class Runner {
  3
  4      public static void main(String[] args) {
  5          CFU4 customInt = new CFU4(5);
  6          customInt.printInt();
  7      }
  8
  9  }
```

```
  CFU4.java  X        *Runner.java
  1
  2  public class CFU4 {
  3
  4      private int myInt = 0;
  5
  6      public CFU4(int change) {
  7          myInt = change;
  8      }
  9
 10      public void printInt() {
 11          System.out.println(myInt);
 12      }
 13
 14  }
```

5. This is when an object is given a state to be in - when an object is created from the keyword "new".

6. Class: System

   Method: println

   Object: out

   Argument: Chapter 4

7. False - The Runner contains the main method and other classes contain the blueprints for actions and objects.

8. True - Classes are written with the first letter capitalized.

Chapter 5: Inheritance

With your knowledge on data types, classes, methods, and more it is time to move on to a more conceptual topic in Java - inheritance. Inheritance refers to the hierarchy of classes that are created in Java, and the transfer of data from one class to another. So how does inheritance work, and why is it helpful?

When we want to create a base set of data and methods in our code, inheritance eliminates redundancy and makes our lives as programmers a lot easier. For example, if we had a class called "Person", we could allow classes of "Student", "Teacher", and "Friend" to **extend** this class. If a Student has properties of a Person, we can allow a Student to inherit what a Person has using the **extends** keyword.

While discussing inheritance, there are a few relationships that you should learn about. First of all, superclasses and subclasses. Superclasses are the classes higher on the hierarchy, the class that gives properties to others. Subclasses are the classes that receive the properties, the ones that are lower on the hierarchy. In the scenario above, the Person class would be a superclass to the Student, Teacher, and Friend classes. The same is true vice versa, saying that Student, Teacher, and Friend are subclasses of Person.

Use the diagram below to understand this simple hierarchy:

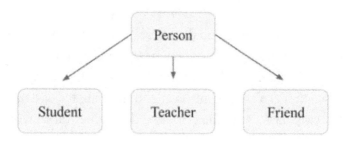

Looking at the diagram, we can see how the arrows show the transfer of data, and the subclasses inheriting the data. When we have a certain class extend another, there are specific attributes it will inherit. Look below to understand what will and will not be inherited in Java (and programming in general).

Subclasses Will Inherit:

Public Variables and Methods - When you declare this public in the superclass, you decide that this can be sent to all the subclasses under said class.

For example, if you had this code in the Person class:

```
public int age = 0;
```

The age variable would travel to the Student class, the Teacher class, and the Friend class. Then, each class could manipulate the variable to their needs.

On the other hand, if the same code was created in one of the subclasses, like the Friend class, then only the Friend class would have that variable. Inheritance is a **one-way relationship.**

When I say variables and methods, there are two types of these - static and instance. Static variables are attached to class properties, while instance variables are attached to certain objects.

Static & Instance Variables and Methods are known as the field, and they are the attributes that are inherited in inheritance. In addition, it must be public. Private variables and methods are not inherited.

Subclasses Will NOT Inherit:

Other than the field, there is almost nothing that subclasses will inherit. Here is a list of a few things that will not be inherited:

Private Variables and Methods - As explained before, the field will only get passed on if it is public and if it is public only. If the word private is anywhere, it is no longer subject to inheritance.

This is very helpful when you have specific variables or methods in a superclass that you do not want a subclass to have access to.

For example, if you have the code below in ANY class -

```
private String name = "I Love Java";
```

It will remain only in the **scope** of that class. Scope refers to how far any type has a jurisdiction to be valid.

Constructors - In addition, to private structures, constructors are never inherited. While it may seem counterintuitive seeing as constructors are public, it is a rule that Java follows. If you have the below constructor in the Person class:

```
public Person(int age) {

    this.age = age;

}
```

Then it will only work in the scope of that class. All of the other classes will have to create their constructors to create executable objects.

```
public Student(int age) {

    this.age = age;

}
```

Example of Inheritance

Let's go through a new project class by class, line by line. Open up your Eclipse and create a new Java Project with the name Inheritance.

Before we get into any analysis, it is important to understand the hierarchy that this project operates in. Let's create a Person class, with 2 classes extending it -

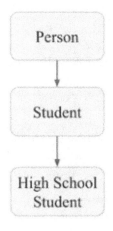

Person is the overall superclass, with Student extending it. Then, High School Student is extending student. This is a 3 tier hierarchy, which will give you a good understanding and learning experience with inheritance.

IS-A Relationships

In order to determine whether a class should extend another or not, there is a specific relationship to bear in mind - the IS-A relationship. The thinking is quite simple: If one class IS another class, then it should extend that class. That very reasoning can be used here.

Let's use a few examples from the examples on the diagram I just gave you:

1. A student is a person

2. A high school student is a student

3. A high school student is a person

From 1 and 2, we see why each class would extend another. In number 3, we see an indirect superclass, where high school student does extend person, just via the student class.

1. A person is not a student

2. A student is not a high school student

From these examples, we see that the classes cannot extend from one another. Inheritance can only be applied if the same is true in all cases. While a person CAN be a student, it is not ALWAYS a student. Therefore, it cannot extend the class.

Breakdown

Type this in your eclipse as we go through it.

Let's start this from the top of the hierarchy - the Person class. We have a normal header like any other class, and we have no main method as that is located in the Runner class that we will create later.

```
public class Person {

}
```

Now, let's think about generic properties that a person would have: A name and a birthday. Just like we did before, let's create 2 instance variables for these actions. Remember that instance variables depend on the object, and our objects here are people. We want these birthdays and names to be different for every object, so instance variables are perfect for this.

Using some reasoning, what data type would cover a name and birthday? A string! Let's declare our variables for this class -

```
private String name;

private String birthday;
```

Next, as a programmer, you should make your constructor. For the sake of this explanation, we will only make one, but if you would like to make more, feel free to.

We created the 2 instance variables previously for the purpose of using them here, so let's place 2 parameters in our constructor. We want to assign these parameters to the empty instance variables we had before. In order to talk about the object we are creating about the variable we are assigning, we use the **this** keyword.

Take a look at this code. If you don't understand the "this" keyword, over time you will, and it is nothing to freak out about.

```
public Person(String name, String
birthday) {

    this.name = name;

    this.birthday = birthday;

}
```

Now, we will create a few instance methods that can return our variables to the Runner class. These methods, whose only purpose is to return certain variables, are called accessor methods.

Let's make 2 accessor methods, one to get the name, and another to get the birthday.

```
public String getName(){

    return name;

}

public String getBirthday() {

    return birthday;

}
```

Notice how the String is in the header, as it is the type that is being returned. Finally, let's create one last instance method that returns the information we need when it is **concatenated.** Concatenation refers to when 2 or more Strings are merged. Time to make this final method.

```
public String toString(){

    return "Name: " + name +
"\nBirthday: "          + birthday;

}
```

Notice how we join together all the strings by using a plus sign, and notice how strings are in quotations while the variables are not. In addition, look at the weird backslash n (\n). This is something called an escape sequence. Some things in Java cannot be blatantly typed out, as Java will take it as an error. Others are shortcuts that allow you to complete easy tasks with the stroke of a letter. Take a look at this list of escape sequences that you could use in the future.

Escape Sequences

\n = New line

\" = Quotation

\\ = Backlash

\r = Return Carriage

\t = Tab

If you want more clarification on escape sequences, search it up and take a look! Here is the completed Person class (next page).

```
  Console ×   Person.java ×
 1  public class Person {
 2
 3      private String name;
 4      private String birthday;
 5
 6      public Person (String name, String birthday)
 7      {
 8          this.name = name;
 9          this.birthday = birthday;
10      }
11
12      public String getName()
13      {
14          return name;
15      }
16
17      public String getBirthday()
18      {
19          return birthday;
20      }
21
22      public String toString()
23      {
24          return "Name: " + name + "\nBirthday: " + birthday;
25      }
26  }
```

Student Class

Now, we will move on to the next class in the hierarchy. Create a new class in your Eclipse project and name it Student. Now, let's start from the header again. Since this class extends another, the header is going to look a bit different. Take a look -

```
public class Student extends Person {

}
```

We use extends, and place the name of the class we are inheriting after. Now, if you recall, we should create some instance variables for this as well. Notice the patterns of writing classes?

What variables should a student have? For this case, we can give them a grade and gpa. Let's declare those variables.

```
private int grade;

private double gpa;
```

As usual, we will make the new constructor as well. Remember, constructors are not inherited, so we will have to create a new one here. We should put the properties of a Person constructor as well as a Student, so let's create a constructor that solves both:

```
public Student (String name, String
birthday, int grade, double gpa) {

        super(name, birthday);

        this.grade = grade;

        this.gpa = gpa;

}
```

Notice the different data types in the parameters, and the use of the **this** keyword once again. However, you may notice something new in this constructor: the **super** keyword. This keyword calls the superclass' constructor and uses the functionality from there. While the subclass does not inherit the constructor, it can still invoke it.

If we trace the code back to the superclass, which in this case is the Person class, we will see that the constructor takes two parameters, which is what we will put in the super call as well. That's why you will notice the code calling the exact requirement needed for that constructor.

```
super(name, birthday);
```

Now, let's create 2 more accessor methods - this should be familiar coding now. the more and more you code, the more patterns and repeating code you will recognize.

```
public int getGrade() {

    return grade;

}

public double getGpa(){

    return gpa;

}
```

Now that we have the accessor methods, instance variables, and constructors created, we can move on to the final class in the hierarchy before creating and finalizing the Runner class.

```java
Student.java  ✕
 1  public class Student extends Person {
 2
 3      private int grade;
 4      private double gpa;
 5
 6      public Student (String name, String birthday, int grade, double gpa)
 7      {
 8          super(name, birthday);
 9          this.grade = grade;
10          this.gpa = gpa;
11      }
12
13      public int getGrade()
14      {
15          return grade;
16      }
17
18      public double getGpa()
19      {
20          return gpa;
21      }
22  }
```

High School Student Class

If you refer back to the diagram, you will notice the last class in this hierarchy is the High School Student class. Using our past terminology, we can identify this as a direct subclass of the Student class and an indirect subclass of the Person class.

Tracing this code line by line, let's remember that we must start with the header. If you recall from the Student class, we must use the extends keyword to inherit the properties from the Student class and Person class.

```
public class HighSchoolStudent extends
Student {

}
```

Once again, it is time to add a variable that would be unique to a High School Student. A variable for volunteering/service hours would be perfect! Time to declare the variable at the top of the class.

```
private int serviceHours;
```

This should be an easy pattern to follow by now, as we have done the same sequence in the past few classes. It is time to create a constructor. However, this time, we need to consider what the superclass's constructor looks like. First, we know that there must be 5 parameters, with the 4 parameter constructor of the Student class in addition to the new instance variable we just created.

```
public HighSchoolStudent(String name,

                String birthday,

                int grade,

                double gpa,

                int serviceHours)
        {

    super(name, birthday, grade, gpa);
```

```
        this.serviceHours = serviceHours;

}
```

While everything looks the same, you may notice that the super call looks a bit different here. While the super call in the Student class had only 2 parameters, this call has 4 - why? This is because the super calls to the direct superclass, which in this case has 4 parameters.

From there, after that constructor is invoked, it calls another super in the Person class, which finally creates the object of a High School Student. Look at each of your constructors and trace through them to understand how this works. The final step in finishing this class is to create the accessor method to return the service hours:

```
public int getServiceHours(){

        return serviceHours;

}
```

```
 1  public class HighSchoolStudent extends Student
 2  {
 3      private int serviceHours;
 4
 5      public HighSchoolStudent(String name, String birthday, int grade,
 6              double gpa, int serviceHours)
 7      {
 8          super(name, birthday, grade, gpa);
 9          this.serviceHours = serviceHours;
10      }
11
12      public int getServiceHours()
13      {
14          return serviceHours;
15      }
16  }
```

Runner Class

To finish off this mini project, we need to create a working running class and the main method. We already start with the main method defaulted, but we should invoke a constructor and create an object. For this example, let's make 2 objects: 1 Person and 1 High School Student. Make sure to use the constructors based on their declarations and parameters -

```
Person myPerson = new Person("Tyler",
"11/12/1999");
```

```
HighSchoolStudent myStudent = new
HighSchoolStudent("Emma", "7/18/2004",
11, 3.9, 65);
```

Now that we have 2 objects declared and instantiated, we can use the accessor methods we created to print information into the console. We will use the same old print statements from before, but call the methods in reference to the objects at the same time.

Let's print some of Emma's information -

```
System.out.println("Student Name: " +
myStudent.getName());
```

```
System.out.println("Grade: " +
myStudent.getGrade());
```

```
System.out.println("Service Hours
Completed: " +
myStudent.getServiceHours());
```

Now, we should have most of Emma's info printed out. If you want to print out other information, make it a challenge, and write an accessor method in the High School Student class that is capable of achieving said functionality.

We created 2 objects, but we only printed out the information of one. Let's print out the information from the Person object, Tyler. Keep in mind that since this is a Person, we can only print either their age or their name. Since we created an accessor method for the name, let's print it to the console.

```
System.out.println("Person Name:" +
myPerson.getName());
```

Go to next page for a visual.

```
1  public class Runner {
2
3▪     public static void main(String[] args) {
4
5          Person myPerson = new Person("Tyler", "11/12/1999");
6          HighSchoolStudent myStudent = new HighSchoolStudent("Emma", "7/18/2004", 11, 3.9, 65);
7          Sophomore rithul = new Sophomore("Rithul", "10/01/2007", 10, 4.0, 55, 25);
8
9          //From Person class
10         System.out.println("Student Name: " + myStudent.getName());
11
12         //From Student class
13         System.out.println("Grade: " + myStudent.getGrade());
14
15         //From HighSchoolStudent class
16         System.out.println("Service Hours Completed: " + myStudent.getServiceHours());
17
18
19         /*
20          * With the person, we only have access to methods from
21          * the Person class.
22          */
23
24         System.out.println("Person Name: " + myPerson.getName());
25     }
26 }
```

```
Console ✕      Runner.java
<terminated> Runner (2) [Java Application] /Users/rit
Student Name: Emma
Grade: 11
Service Hours Completed: 65
Person Name: Tyler
```

Check For Understanding (Chapter 5)

1. What is the name of the keyword that allows a class to become a subclass and inherit the properties from its superclass?

2. What is the keyword to invoke a constructor?

3. Create another class in addition to the example given to you in the chapter. Name it Sophomore. The Sophomore class should extend to High School Students.

4. Give the class an instance variable of classRank. Then, create a constructor with 6 parameters, and assign the variable of classRank to whatever is placed in the argument. Finally, create an accessor method to return the value of classRank.

5. In the Runner class, create an object of Sophomore with the extra property of Class Rank. Then, print out the information in the console.

6. Draw a diagram to show the new hierarchy in our project.

7. True or False: Inheritance is a double-sided relationship. Both subclasses and superclasses inherit properties from each other.

8. True or False: Subclasses cannot inherit private methods.

9. True or False: When you call the super keyword, it invokes the constructor at the top of the entire class hierarchy.

Check For Understanding (Chapter 5 ANSWERS)

1. extends

2. new

3. It is normal to have an error here. (red line under Sophomore)

```
Console    Runner.java    *Sophomore.java ×
1  public class Sophomore extends HighSchoolStudent
2  {
3  |
4  }
```

4. All errors should be gone here. Notice the same pattern that was followed in this class that was the same case in others.

```
Console    Runner.java    Sophomore.java ×
 1  public class Sophomore extends HighSchoolStudent
 2  {
 3      private int classRank;
 4
 5      public Sophomore(String name, String birthday, int grade,
 6              double gpa, int serviceHours, int classRank)
 7      {
 8          super(name, birthday, grade, gpa, serviceHours);
 9          this.classRank = classRank;
10      }
11
12      public int getClassRank()
13      {
14          return classRank;
15      }
16  }
```

Notice how all of the parameters stayed the same from the High School Student, except now we added an extra parameter for our new instance variable.

Take a look at the super call - notice how it is changed so that it properly calls the constructor of the Sophomore class's direct superclass - High School Student.

5. In the Runner class, we create the object on line 7, and then all the other information is after like 26. Notice how each of the lines calls a different aspect of the sophomore, before printing all the information to the console.

```java
public class Runner {

    public static void main(String[] args) {

        Person myPerson = new Person("Tyler", "11/12/1999");
        HighSchoolStudent myStudent = new HighSchoolStudent("Emma", "7/18/2004", 11, 3.9, 65);
        Sophomore stuart = new Sophomore("Stuart", "02/08/2008", 10, 3.7, 20, 235);

        //From Person class
        System.out.println("Student Name: " + myStudent.getName());

        //From Student class
        System.out.println("Grade: " + myStudent.getGrade());

        //From HighSchoolStudent class
        System.out.println("Service Hours Completed: " + myStudent.getServiceHours());

        /*
         * With the person, we only have access to methods from
         * the Person class.
         */

        System.out.println("Person Name: " + myPerson.getName());


        // Start printing Sophomore information here:

        System.out.println("Sophomore Name: " + stuart.getName());
        System.out.println("Sophomore Bday: " + stuart.getBirthday());
        System.out.println("Sophomore Grade: " + stuart.getGrade());
        System.out.println("Sophomore GPA: " + stuart.getGpa());
        System.out.println("Sophomore Service Hours: " + stuart.getServiceHours());
        System.out.println("Sophomore Rank in Class: " + stuart.getClassRank());
    }
}
```

```
Console X    CFU.java    Sopt
<terminated> Runner (2) [Java Application] /Us
Student Name: Emma
Grade: 11
Service Hours Completed: 65
Person Name: Tyler
Sophomore Name: Stuart
Sophomore Bday: 02/08/2008
Sophomore Grade: 10
Sophomore GPA: 3.7
Sophomore Service Hours: 20
Sophomore Rank in Class: 235
```

Check For Understanding (Chapter 5 ANSWERS Cont.)

6.

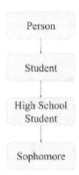

7. False - Only subclasses inherit the properties of the superclass. Inheritance is a one-way relationship.

8. True - Once a method or variable is made private, it cannot be transferred to another class. Inheritance only works with public structures. Notice all the accessor methods in our project - they are all public. This is why the Sophomore class has access to all of them.

9. False - When you call the super keyword, it invokes the constructor of the direct superclass. Once again, refer to the chapter project for reference. For every constructor we created for each subsequent subclass, we altered the call to the super so that it perfectly fits the description of the constructor in the class directly above it.

Chapter 6: Polymorphism

In addition to Inheritance is yet another crucial OOP concept - Polymorphism. Breaking down the word for its literal meaning, "poly-" meaning many and "-morphism" being the act of changing something, this concept relates back to the redundancy of code and how to minimize it.

Polymorphism allows for usage of the same method name, but different method actions. This may seem extremely confusing when phrased like that, so here is an example of a step-by-step programmer point of view (POV) of how polymorphism works. This shows how a programmer would incorporate Polymorphism in their code:

1. A superclass of Person creates a method of "Sleep", which prints out the time that the average person goes to bed every night, around 11:00 (pm).

2. A subclass of Person, called Coder, is created. Just like the Person class, Coder also has a Sleep method. A coder sleeps at 12:30 (am).

3. Two objects are created in the Runner Class, one Person and one Coder. When the Sleep method is called for both objects, it prints 11:00 for the Person, but 12:30 for the Coder.

From the example, you will notice that polymorphism occurs alongside inheritance, which is why you must understand how inheritance works.

In polymorphism, the same method name is taken into different classes, and each class changes the method function to however it is best suited for the class functionality.

In the example, the Sleep method is used in both classes, however, the classes morph the output into different values upon the call of the method. There are 2 main concepts surrounding methods you need to know: overriding and overloading. Each has its advantages.

Overriding Methods

Overriding occurs when the same method is used word for word - with the only difference between methods being that the body is different. This means that the header and the name of the method are the same, in addition to the number of parameters that are in the method as well.

Here is an example of a method override. The Age class will be a superclass for the Child, Teen, Adult, and Senior classes. The Age class creates its own "ageRange" method, however, this method is overridden in every other class to the values that it should print.

Breakdown

Just like any other breakdown, let's start with the class at the top of the hierarchy - the Age class. Here's another diagram if you need a visual.

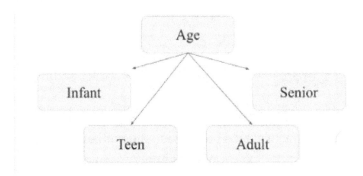

Age Class

The code is quite simple from class to class. We have the default header, and then one instance method in the body. The instance method, named ageRange, prints a statement to the console saying that the overall range is from 0-100. Keep in mind we retain the same name of the method throughout all the classes.

```
Age.java ✕
1
2 public class Age {
3
4⊖    public void ageRange() {
5        System.out.println("Age ranges from 0-100");
6    }
7
8 }
```

Child Class

This is one of the 4 subclasses of Age, so it should extend that class. Now, we need to override the method so that it displays the correct age range for children. In order to override, we need to keep all the details the same - except for the print statement itself. Obviously, age ranges vary in real life, but for the sake of this example, follow the ranges included. First, we will make the ageRange function print 0-12 for any Child object.

```
*Child.java ✕
1
2 public class Child extends Age{
3⊖    public void ageRange() {
4        System.out.println("Child ranges from 0-12");
5    }
6 }
7
```

Teen, Adult, & Senior Classes

The same principle from the Child class can be applied here to these classes. We extend the Age class and then change the print statement in the ageRange method to print out 13-19 for Teens, 18-65 for Adults, and 65-100 for Seniors.

```java
public class Teen extends Age{
    public void ageRange() {
        System.out.println("Teen ranges from 13-19");
    }
}
```

```java
public class Adult extends Age{
    public void ageRange() {
        System.out.println("Adult ranges from 20-65");
    }
}
```

```java
public class Senior extends Age{
    public void ageRange() {
        System.out.println("Senior ranges from 65-100");
    }
}
```

Runner Class

Like any other Runner class we have done in the past, we have the default header and main method in our file. In the first 5 lines, we create objects for all of the classes. If you look closely, there is something different about these instantiations. Usually, when we want to create a Child, we would write

```
Child myChild = new Child();
```

However, now that we want to incorporate polymorphism, we place the Child's superclass, Age, at the front instead. This means that the object will only receive commands that an Age object could take. However, polymorphism will take this command and change the output to what an Child's age range would be. In this case, the only command that an Age object would take is "ageRange", which is why the output changes in the console.

For the rest of the objects, we follow the same pattern, by putting the superclass of Age in the front of the instantiation for polymorphism. If we used our knowledge from previous constructor invoking lines, it would look like this:

```
Child myChild = new Child();

Teen myTeen = new Teen();

Adult myAdult = new Adult();
```

Senior mySenior = new Senior();

Age myAge = new Age();

However, now that we want to incorporate polymorphism and only allow these specific objects to follow Age commands, the new code looks like the code in the Runner class.

Age myChild = new Child();

Age myTeen = new Teen();

Age myAdult = new Adult();

Age mySenior = new Senior();

Age myAge = new Age();

```java
public class Runner {

    public static void main(String[] args) {
        Age myChild = new Child();
        Age myTeen = new Teen();
        Age myAdult = new Adult();
        Age mySenior = new Senior();
        Age myAge = new Age();

        myChild.ageRange();
        myTeen.ageRange();
        myAdult.ageRange();
        mySenior.ageRange();
        myAge.ageRange();;
    }

}
```

Now that all of our objects are created, we simply call the ageRange function for all the objects. Take a look at the console and notice how each output is completely different because of the polymorphism!

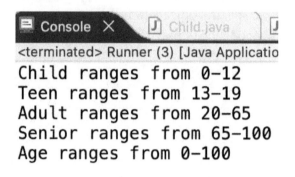

Console X   Child.java
<terminated> Runner (3) [Java Applicatio
Child ranges from 0-12
Teen ranges from 13-19
Adult ranges from 20-65
Senior ranges from 65-100
Age ranges from 0-100

Overloading Methods

Overloading is similar to overriding, but has different intentions with the code itself. Unlike how overriding must have the same head, overloading requires that you have the same name, but different parameters.

This either means you have a different data type (returning int instead of double), or you have a different number of parameters (2 ints instead of 1). The reason you need these different parameters is because, with the same name, the code will error without any way to contrast the two methods.

Take a look at the example below that relates to overloading. Remember to **write all examples along with the book in Eclipse** either when you see the **images** or in the **breakdown**. Typing the code yourself helps a lot in **retaining** information!

For the following example, we will create an example relating to vehicles. We will write our code in the same class, but comment out the other code in the main method in order to run the hierarchy we want when we execute our program.

Hierarchy Diagram

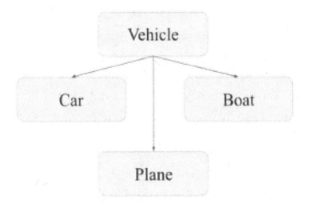

Vehicle Class

Just like any other class, we have our default header. Then, we create an instance method - at this point, you should be familiar with the syntax and logic surrounding instance methods.

The method, called horsepower, is programmed so that it prints out a generic statement related to horsepower with vehicles, which is that they can vary!

```java
public class Vehicle {
    public void horsepower() {
        System.out.println("A vehicle can vary in HP");
    }
}
```

Car Class

Now that we are handling a subclass, the Car class's header contains the extends keyword, allowing the Vehicle class to be its direct superclass. Inside the body of the class itself, we will create 2 instance methods. This is where overloading takes place.

If we were to override the method here, we would have no parameters in our method and the header would look like this (next page):

```
public void horsepower()
```

Instead, for overloading, we want to change the parameter values. We will make one instance method take one int as a parameter, while the second one will take one double as a parameter.

```
Vehicle.java    Car.java  X    Plane.java    Bolt.java    Runner.java    Console
 1 |
 2 public class Car extends Vehicle{
 3     public void horsepower(int d) {
 4         System.out.println("A car could have " + d + " HP");
 5     }
 6
 7     public void horsepower(double e) {
 8         System.out.println("A car could have " + e + " HP");
 9     }
10 }
```

If you look at the example images, you will see this implementation. Now, for the body of these methods, we want to create a contrast between the default method and these overloaded methods, so we will make the parameters print in the console.

To add some cleanliness to it, we will make it into a sentence that concatenates the integer and doubles into the statement.

Plane Class

Just like the Car class, a plane IS A vehicle, so we will extend the class in the header.

Since we already created 2 overloaded methods in the Car class, we will just create one here.

To change the parameter constraints once again, let's make it a String that is once again concatenated to the final print statement.

If you notice, it is the same pattern repeatedly with the instance methods - a new class with inheritance, and nearly the same instance variables with just a different parameter list.

```java
public class Plane extends Vehicle{
    public void horsepower(String d) {
        System.out.println("A plane could have " + d + " HP");
    }
}
```

Boat Class

With the same pattern as the other subclasses, we extend Vehicle and overload the horsepower method. In this method, we will take as long as the parameter and print it in the console.

```
1
2 public class Boat extends Vehicle{
3     public void horsepower(long d) {
4         System.out.println("A boat could have " + d + " HP");
5     }
6 }
7
```

Runner Class

The first thing we want to do in the Runner class comments out all the other code from the overriding example. This will make sure we are running the right code. You can do multiline comments with "/*" to start and "*/" to end.

We create 4 different objects, one per class, in the constructor. Make sure that the type before the equals sign is the same as the type after. For example, if we were overriding, the object instantiations would look like this:

```
Vehicle myCar = new Car();

Vehicle myCar = new Plane();

Vehicle myCar = new Boat();

Vehicle myCar = new Vehicle();
```

Now, it should be the same on each statement itself.

Just like any other Runner, we will call methods upon the objects in order to see the output in the console. In the example, I printed every single possible horsepower method for each object, which is 3 for a car, 3 for a boat and plane, and just 1 for a vehicle.

Take a look at the next page for the complete Runner class:

```java
1
2  public class Runner {
3
4    public static void main(String[] args) {
5        /*Age myInfant = new Infant();
6        Age myTeen = new Teen();
7        Age myAdult = new Adult();
8        Age mySenior = new Senior();
9        Age myAge = new Age();
10
11       myInfant.ageRange();
12       myTeen.ageRange();
13       myAdult.ageRange();
14       mySenior.ageRange();
15       myAge.ageRange();*/
16
17       Car myCar = new Car();
18       Plane myPlane = new Plane();
19       Boat myBoat = new Boat();
20       Vehicle myVehicle = new Vehicle();
21
22       myCar.horsepower();
23       myCar.horsepower(250);
24       myCar.horsepower(315.3);
25       myPlane.horsepower("2000");
26       myPlane.horsepower();
27       myBoat.horsepower(2000L);
28       myBoat.horsepower();
29       myVehicle.horsepower();
30
31    }
32
33 }
```

The methods will print into the console respective of the different parameters they take and the output that is produced from those parameters.

```
<terminated> Runner (3) [Java Application] /Use
A vehicle can vary in HP
A car could have 250 HP
A car could have 315.3 HP
A plane could have 2000 HP
A vehicle can vary in HP
A boat could have 2000 HP
A vehicle can vary in HP
A vehicle can vary in HP
```

Now that you have finished Inheritance and Polymorphism, you are just a concept away from the trifecta in Object Oriented Programming. The last stop: Encapsulation!

Encapsulation

After everything you have learned, encapsulation is actually quite a simple concept. All it refers to is the binding of the data, variables, and methods between your classes and how you handle them. Whether you use public or private keywords, etc, you are controlling the scope of those variables/methods and where they can go. This control that you have establishes borders, or rather encapsulates, these methods and variables in your program.

Take a look at this quick example to see what encapsulation looks like (next page):

```
Main.java  ✕
1
2  public class Main {
3
4⊖      public void printHi() {
5             System.out.println("Hi");
6         }
7
8⊖      public static void main(String[] args) {
9
10            int x = 5;
11            System.out.println(x);
12
13         }
14
15  }
```

When we glance at this code, we can see all the encapsulation relationships that are taking place. First of all, all of the code in this image is encapsulated within the Main Class.

Then, the printHi() method is encapsulated, or has the scope, of everything in the Main class. The variable x, however, is only located in the main method. It is encapsulated from inside that method, and therefore, cannot be called outside of it.

Check For Understanding (Chapter 6)

1. What is method overriding?

2. What is method overloading?

3. True or False: Polymorphism goes perfectly with inheritance.

4. Think of a real world example that relates to polymorphism other than the ones that were included in this chapter.

5. Write your own example of an overriding/overloading hierarchy with 3 classes and a Runner.

Check For Understanding (Chapter 6 ANSWERS)

1. Overriding a method occurs when the exact same method details are used to call the same method name while producing a different output.

2. Overloading a method occurs when the same method name is used while different parameter lists are declared, meaning the same method can be used for different outputs.

3. True - Everything related to polymorphism would not be possible without inheritance.

4. Answers can vary.... Just make sure that there is some relationship between events you are referencing. An example could be having an animal (name, age). Then, there could be separate methods and features for different types of animals (mammals, reptiles, insects, etc.).

5. It is up to you on what to create! Building off of my example, you could extend the Animal and other classes for different methods and actions.

Chapter 7: Control Flow

Now that we covered all of the important theoretical concepts in Java, there is one more concept, which is more practical, that you should learn. Control flow relates to how you change data based on variables that may change throughout your program. In Java, there are different ways to use control flow, but the main methods are:

1. If statements

2. For loops

3. While loops

These vary in the way they are written, and each of them has their own advantages. Throughout this chapter we will go through each of them and at the end you will decide which loop/statement you prefer.

One thing to understand about each of these loops is that they have different forms of syntax, and that they are more powerful when incorporated within methods and called multiple times.

If Statements

An if statement is structured so that IF something happens, then some code is triggered. If it doesn't happen, or something ELSE happens, then another segment of code is triggered.

When we look at the syntax of if statements, it has a similar pattern to other Java structures: your generic header, and then the body with the code segments inside. The header will have the keyword if, and then the actual **condition** in the parenthesis. The condition is whatever has to return true for the code to execute.

```
if(condition) {

}
```

This is an example of a bare-bones if statement. The header has the if statement, and a condition in the parenthesis immediately after.

Create a new Eclipse project called Control Flow. Inside, make a class called Main. Since we are testing out small segments of code in this chapter, it won't be necessary to have a separate Runner class. Make sure to include the main method as a default.

Now that we have our default Main class and main method, we can write our if statement inside. In this example, let's create a condition checking for whether a variable of type int is set to the value of 7.

We know that before accessing or manipulating any variables, we must declare them. Let's declare and initialize an int to a value of 7.

```
int value = 7;
```

Now that we have a variable, we can check it using the conditions in an if statement. Let's write an if statement header like the one I showed you before. Let's verify whether "value" is equal to the value of 7.

```
if(value == 7){

}
```

If you notice, we do not write "value = 7" as the condition, but we write "value == 7". This is because the "=" is known as the assignment operator, so all it will do is assign the value of 7 to value. In order to see if they are holding the same value, we must use the double equal sign, or "==".

Now that we have a skeleton for the if statement, we can add in the content. If we see that value is 7, then we can print "The value is 7!" to the console. Let's place that in our statement.

```
if (value == 7) {

    System.out.println("The value is
7!");

}
```

So, we now have an action IF value = 7, but what if it isn't? Now, we should add the "else" keyword to make the code do something if the value of value is anything except 7. For this, all we do is write else, add a set of brackets, and place our functionality inside. Let's make the else segment print "The value is NOT 7!".

```
if (value == 7) {

    System.out.println("The value is
7!");

} else {

    System.out.println("The value is
NOT 7!");

}
```

Now, if we run the code, we should see that the console has "They are the same" printed. Now, if we change the value of "value" to 8, see what prints in the console - "They are different".

This is the basics of if statements. In the future, when you want to test more complicated things, if statements will be incredibly useful!

For Loops

While the if statements are good at checking the status and condition of things in our code, loops play a key role when we want to **iterate** through multiple things. Iteration refers to when we repeat the same action over and over again, whether it is mathematical, through a list, etc.

Instead of writing redundant lines of code to add 1 to a number and print it the console x number of times, a for loop will allow you to do it in just 4! For the syntax in a for loop, we write the for keyword. Then, we declare and initialize a variable and iterate through it.

```
for (int x = 0; x < 5; x++) {

}
```

When you look at this barebones for loop, notice a few things. First of all, we declare and initialize the int of x in the parenthesis.

After the first semicolon, we say that this loop should run when x is less than 5. Finally, we say that after every iteration of the loop, we will increase x by 1 count. Essentially, this loop will run 5 times.

You can alter these conditions to more specific variables in the future, but for now this is all you need to know.

Now that we established the loop specifications, we write what we want the loop to go through on every iteration inside the loop. Let's make a for loop together now.

We want to first establish how many times our loop will iterate. For this example, we will make it iterate 20 times. Looking at the patterns from the previous example I gave you, it should be simple that the loop header looks like this:

```
for (int x = 0; x < 20; x++) {

}
```

Now, we should create some functionality. Let's create an int named count that we increment by 1 every single time that a for loop iterates. Start by declaring and initializing the variable above the for loop.

```
int count = 0;
```

Inside the for loop itself, let's make the count variable increase by 1. Then, let's print it to the console so that we can see it progress through the loop when we run the program.

```
for (int x = 0; x < 20; x++) {

    count = count + 1;

    System.out.println(count);

}
```

Your class should look something like this:

```
1
2  public class Main {
3
4⊖     public static void main(String[] args) {
5          int value = 8;
6
7          if(value == 7) {
8              System.out.println("The value is 7!");
9          } else {
10             System.out.println("The value is NOT 7!");
11         }
12
13         int count = 0;
14
15         for (int x = 0; x <  20; x++) {
16             count = count + 1;
17             System.out.println(count);
18         }
19     }
20 }
```

Now that we have written everything needed, we can run the program. It should result in all numbers from 1-20 getting printed in the console. You can see how this is extremely helpful - 20 lines of output were created from 4-5 lines of code!

While Loops

Now that we have created for loops, creating while loops should be a breeze. While for loops have a set number of iterations, "while loops" continue running UNTIL the condition is false. For example, it will continue running UNTIL an integer is not greater than 70.

Regarding syntax, the while loop is quite simple. You just add the while keyword, your condition after, and then the actions of the loop in the brackets.

```
while(condition){

}
```

Let's create a while loop that is similar to the for loop. Looking at the barebones structure, you may notice a few patterns in the syntax of the code. In the Main class, comment out the for loop as well. Let's make a while loop that decrements from 100 all the way to 70.

The first thing we would have to do is declare and initialize a variable with the value of 100.

```
int num = 100;
```

Now, let's create the skeleton of our while loop. We know that we want to iterate until num is equal to 70, so the loop should run WHILE num is greater than 70.

```
while(num > 70){

}
```

Now, it is time to put our functionality in the body of the while loop.

We already established that we want the value of num to decrease until it hits 70. We also want to print this value to the console so that we can iterate it through the loop as it iterates.

```
while(num > 70){

    num = num - 1;

    System.out.println(num);

}
```

If we run our program, we should get every number from 70-100, but printed backwards. Notice how the while and for loops work very similarly and have similar output as well. Sooner or later, you will choose which one you want to use based on your personal needs and preferences.

```java
public class Main {

    public static void main(String[] args) {
        int value = 8;

        if(value == 7) {
            System.out.println("They are the same!");
        } else {
            System.out.println("They are different!");
        }

        int count = 0;

        for (int x = 0; x <  20; x++) {
            count = count + 1;
            System.out.println(count);
        }

        int num = 100;

        while(num > 70) {
            num = num - 1;
            System.out.println(num);
        }

    }
}
```

Check For Understanding (Chapter 7)

1. What is the benefit of a loop?

2. What are the 2 types of loops that we discussed in this chapter?

3. Declare and initialize a variable of type String. Initialize the value to "I like coding".

4. Write an if statement that checks if the value of a String is "I like java".

5. Write a "for" AND "while" loop to iterate all numbers from 1-100 and print them in the console.

Check For Understanding (Chapter 7 ANSWERS)

1. Loops make it very easy to code repetitive segments of code

2. For and While loops

3. Look at lines 5

4. Look at lines 6-11 (Should print out "They are different")

5. Look at lines 13-25 (Should print all values 1-100)

```java
1
2  public class CFU {
3
4⊝     public static void main(String[] args) {
5          String condition = "I like coding";
6
7          if(condition == "I like java") {
8              System.out.println("They are the same!");
9          } else {
10             System.out.println("They are different!");
11         }
12
13         int count = 0;
14
15         for (int x = 0; x <  100; x++) {
16             count = count + 1;
17             System.out.println(count);
18         }
19
20         int num = 0;
21
22         while(num < 100) {
23             num = num + 1;
24             System.out.println(num);
25         }
26
27     }
28
29 }
```

Chapter 8: Miscellaneous

The purpose of this chapter is to briefly cover some topics that will help you. If you want to explore these concepts more, feel free to search it up and learn it.

Wrapper Classes

Wrapper classes are the name of the classes that wrap around our primitive types. Remember the 8 primitives we went over previously? They each have a class that holds them. These classes are automatically included in Java files, which is why primitives do not have to be imported. Here is the list of the 8 primitives and their respective wrapper classes.

boolean - Boolean

byte - Byte

short - Short

int - Integer

float - Float

long - Long

double - Double

char - Character

Notice how they are basically the same, but with a capital letter. These are the naming conventions, which we will now discuss.

Naming Conventions

When it comes to naming so many different things in Java, there are certain rules you should follow to make it easier for you and your team member's code easier to understand. Here is a basic breakdown of common Java structures and how you should name them.

When it comes to naming classes, it is always good practice to start with a capital letter and then use camelCase for every additional word.

Example: MyClass

When you want to name variables, you should use a lowercase letter and then camelCase.

Example: myVariable

For methods, you should use the same conventions as variables, with the first word lowercase and then camelCase.

Example: myMethod

When you want to use constants, write in all CAPS and use something called snake_case, where you put underscores in between every word. A constant is a variable that cannot be changed once it has been given a value. It is **immutable**.

Example: MY_CONSTANT

Randomization

In addition to the simple math operations that you were taught earlier in the book, there is also a Math class that you can import. With the import, there are a variety of functions that you can use, but the most commonly used is the random function.

You can do this on your own, as it is quite simple. Create a main method class, and import math(lang class) at the top. Then, browse through the different functions, specifically the random function.

You can use the random function to generate any random number within the range that you give it. This is helpful for you to create a simple guessing game. Use if statements to check if the user is right, and use a while loop to continue the game until the user wins.

User Input

We have done so much work with coding and how to manipulate variables that we have created, but what about a user? User input is very common to use in programs, so it only makes sense that you learn about it in Java as well.

In order to allow for Java input, you must input a class called Scanner. Scanner is inside a library called Utilities, so you would import it like this.

```
import java.util.Scanner;
```

Now, you have to declare and instantiate the call to the Scanner. Then, you print out your question or prompt. Finally, grab the user's input and store it in a variable.

```
Scanner myInput = new
Scanner(System.in);

System.out.println("What is your
name?");

String name = myInput.nextLine();
```

Now, you can use this input however you would like.

```
 1  import java.util.Scanner;
 2
 3  public class Misc {
 4
 5⊖     public static void main(String[] args) {
 6          Scanner myInput = new Scanner(System.in);
 7          System.out.println("What is your name?");
 8          String name = myInput.nextLine();
 9
10
11      }
12
13  }
```

Karel J Robot

I don't have instructions for this section, but just a helpful
tool. If you feel you want a better understanding of
polymorphism, inheritance, etc, using the Karel J Robot
software is a great way to go. The physical robots and the
way they move throughout the world give a nice visual to
understand what is happening in the code. Search up the
name online and get started if you are interested.

Chapter 9: Glossary

Argument/Parameter: Values passed to a function or method.

Assignment: Giving a value to a variable.

Break: Terminates a loop or switch statement.

Braces: Curly brackets used to group statements.

Brackets: Symbols "[" and "]" used for grouping and indexing.

Bytecode: Intermediate code between source code and machine code.

Case: A condition in a switch statement.

Comment: Non-executable text to explain code.

Concatenation: Combining strings or data.

Continue: Skips the rest of a loop's code and starts the next iteration.

Declaration: Introducing a variable with its type.

Do While Loop: Executes a block of code while a condition is true.

Extends: Indicates inheritance in object-oriented programming.

Field: A variable within a class.

Final: A keyword indicating that a variable or method cannot be modified.

For Loop: Repeats a block of code a specific number of times.

Garbage Collector: Automatically frees up memory by removing unused objects.

If Statement: Conditional execution of code.

Immutable: Unchangeable or constant.

Inheritance: A mechanism for creating a new class based on an existing one.

Initialization: Assigning an initial value to a variable.

Instance: An individual occurrence of an object.

Iteration: Repeating a set of statements in a loop.

JDK: Java Development Kit, a software development kit for Java.

JAR: Java Archive, a file format used to aggregate many Java class files.

Main Method: The entry point for Java applications.

Modulus: Returns the remainder of a division operation.

New: Creates a new instance of a class.

Null: Represents the absence of a value.

Object: An instance of a class in object-oriented programming.

OOP: Object-Oriented Programming, a programming paradigm based on objects.

Operator: Symbols used for operations like addition or comparison.

Overloading: Defining multiple methods with the same name but different parameters.

Overriding: Providing a specific implementation for a method in a subclass.

Parenthesis: Symbols "(" and ")" used to group expressions or parameters.

Polymorphism: The ability of a class to take on multiple forms.

Private: Access modifier restricting visibility to within the class.

Public: Access modifier allowing visibility from any other class.

Recursion: A function calling itself during its execution.

Reference: Memory address pointing to the location of an object.

Reassignment: Giving a new value to an existing variable.

Return: Sends a value back from a function.

Scope: The region of the code where a variable is valid.

Statement (Statement Terminator): Represents an action or command. A terminator is a semicolon (;)

Static: Belonging to the class rather than an instance of the class.

String: A sequence of characters.

Subclass: A class that inherits from another class.

Super: Refers to the superclass in object-oriented programming.

Superclass: The class from which a subclass is derived.

Terminal: An interface for interacting with a computer.

This: Refers to the current instance of an object.

Try: Encloses a block of code in which exceptions may occur.

Void: Denotes that a method does not return any value.

Wrapper Class: Converts primitive data types into objects.

While Loop: Repeats a block of code while a condition is true.

Closing Remarks

Thank you so much for reading this book! I tried my best to outline all the Java concepts in an easy-to-understand manner, and I hope you gained something from it!

Please continue to explore and learn Java as well as other programming languages. Expand your knowledge and apply it!

Once again, thank you.

-    Rithul Bhat